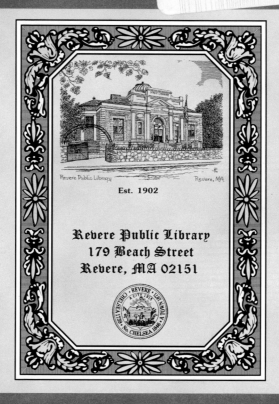

Creativity

A Short and Cheerful Guide

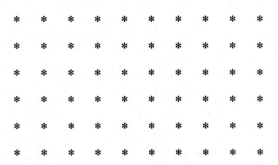

Creativity

A Short and Cheerful Guide

John Cleese

CROWN
NEW YORK

Published in the United States by Crown, an imprint of
Random House, a division of Penguin Random House LLC,
New York. Simultaneously published in hardcover in Great
Britain by Hutchinson, an imprint of Cornerstone, a division of
Penguin Random House Ltd., London.

CROWN and the Crown colophon are registered trademarks of
Penguin Random House LLC.

Hardback ISBN 978-0-385-34827-0
Ebook ISBN 978-0-385-34828-7

Printed in the United States of America on acid-free paper

crownpublishing.com

987654321

First Edition

Book design by Tim Barnes, herechickychicky.com

Contents

*   *   *   *   *   *   *   *   *   *

*   *   *   *   *   *   *   *   *   *

*   *   *   *   *   *   *   *   *   *

*   *   *   *   *   *   *   *   *   *

*   *   *   *   *   *   *   *   *   *

*   *   *   *   *   *   *   *   *   *

*   *   *   *   *   *   *   *   *   *

*   *   *   *   *   *   *   *   *   *

*   *

*   *   *Introduction*

*   *

*   *   *   *   *   *   *   *   *   *

*   *   *   *   *   *   *   *   *   *

*   *   *   *   *   *   *   *   *   *

*   *   *   *   *   *   *   *   *   *

*   *   *   *   *   *   *   *   *   *

*   *   *   *   *   *   *   *   *   *

*   *   *   *   *   *   *   *   *   *

*   *   *   *   *   *   *   *   *   *

by creativity, I simply mean new ways of thinking about things.

Most people think of creativity as being entirely about the arts—music, painting, theatre, movies, dancing, sculpture, etc., etc.

But this simply isn't so. Creativity can be seen in every area of life—in science, or in business, or in sport.

Wherever you can find a way of doing things that is better than what has been done before, you are being creative.

Another myth is that creativity is something you have to be born with. This isn't the case. Anyone can be creative.

When I was at school in the late forties and the fifties, no teacher ever mentioned the word creativity. Just think how extraordinary that is.

Mind you, this was partly because I did Science at school—my A levels were in Maths, Physics and Chemistry—and, of course, there wasn't much room for me to be creative in those subjects.

You have to learn an awful lot of science before you can even begin to think about taking a creative approach to it.

Then I went to Cambridge and studied Law. Not much creativity there. You just had to decide whether one particular set of facts fell into this category or that category.

But, regardless of the subjects I chose to study, it's clear that nobody in charge of the English education system seemed to have realised there was any need to teach creativity.

And you *can* teach creativity. Or perhaps I should say, more accurately,

you can teach people how to create cir-
cumstances in which they will *become*
creative.

And that's what this little book is
all about.

*	*	*	*	*	*	*	*	*	*
*	*	*	*	*	*	*	*	*	*
*	*	*	*	*	*	*	*	*	*
*	*	*	*	*	*	*	*	*	*
*	*	*	*	*	*	*	*	*	*
*	*	*	*	*	*	*	*	*	*
*	*	*	*	*	*
*	*	*	*	*	*	*The**e*
*
*	*Creative**ve*
*
*	**Mindset**t*
*	*
*	*	*	*	*	*	*	*	*	*
*	*	*	*	*	*	*	*	*	*
*	*	*	*	*	*	*	*	*	*
*	*	*	*	*	*	*	*	*	*
*	*	*	*	*	*	*	*	*	*
*	*	*	*	*	*	*	*	*	*

***the* first time I discovered I was a bit creative, it came as a surprise**. I was at Cambridge and I had got to know a very nice group of people who had a small club room near my digs, as they were a part of a society called the "Footlights." They put on little shows on the club-room stage, performing sketches and monologues and musical items.

I didn't join the Footlights because I thought I might want to go into show business. Not at all! I was going to be a lawyer! I joined the club because its members were the nicest bunch of people I met at Cambridge. They were good company—of course, since they were all in one way or another funny— and they were also an interesting mixture of social classes and academic interests. For some reason—maybe because they had a sense of humour— they weren't stuck up, or show-offs, or in any way impressed with themselves.

To become a member of the Footlights you first had to write something. I therefore came up with a couple of sketches to perform, and was accepted.

Each month, I discovered, they organised what was known as a "smoker"—short for the old-fashioned phrase "smoking concert." This was a show put on in the Footlights' club room in which all members took part. Because everyone had to get up and do something, we all had an interest in creating a nice, friendly atmosphere, so it was the perfect environment if you were performing for the first time.

And it was during the course of writing sketches—the first imaginative thing I was ever conscious of doing—that I realised that I could be "creative." That is to say, if I wrote something down on a piece of paper, and performed it later on, I could make people laugh. And the point is . . . what I was writing was original. (I don't mean that I wasn't influenced by lots of other people and comedy programmes I thought wonderful—especially *The Goon Show*—but what was going down on the paper was . . . *mine*.)

And then I started becoming aware of something else that was interesting. And very odd, too.

If I wrote a sketch by myself in the evening, I'd often get stuck, and would sit there at my little desk, cudgeling my brains. Eventually I'd give up and go to bed.

And in the morning, I'd wake up and

make myself a cup of coffee, and then I'd drift over to the desk and sit at it, and, almost immediately, the solution to the problem I'd been wrestling with the previous evening . . . became quite obvious to me! So obvious that I couldn't really understand why I hadn't spotted it the night before. But I hadn't.

This is how I began to discover that, **if I put the work in before going to bed**, **I often had a little creative idea overnight**, which fixed whatever problem it was that I was trying to deal with. It was like a gift, a reward for all my wrestling with the puzzle. I began to think to myself, "It can only be that while I'm asleep, my mind goes on working at the problem so that it can give me the answer in the morning."

This realisation was very foreign to me. I had always assumed that thinking was all about furrowing my brow, and trying terribly hard.

While I was still wondering about this, something else occurred.

I sometimes collaborated with my friend Graham Chapman, and we had written a parody of a Church of England sermon. (At that time Graham and I were both obsessed with all the humour we could derive from the Bible: so much so that when people came into my room and saw an

Authorised Version on my desk, they would say, "Oh! You've been writing sketches again.")

Graham and I thought it was rather a good sketch. It was therefore terribly embarrassing when I found I'd lost it. I knew Graham was going to be cross, so when I'd given up looking for it, I sat down and rewrote the whole thing from memory. It actually turned out to be easier than I'd expected.

Then I found the original sketch and, out of curiosity, checked to see how well I'd recalled it when rewriting. Weirdly, I discovered that the remembered version was actually an improvement on the one that Graham and I had written. This puzzled the hell out of me.

Again I was forced to the conclusion that my mind must have continued to think about the sketch after Graham and I had finished it. And that my mind had been improving what we'd written, without my making any conscious attempt to do so. So when I remembered it, it was already better.

Chewing this over, I realised it was like the tip-of-the-tongue phenomenon: when you can't remember a name, and you chase after it in your mind, and find you just cannot recall it . . . and then a few moments later, when you are thinking about something else, the name pops into your mind. Clearly, your brain was still working on it even after you'd given up.

So I began to realise that **my unconscious was working on stuff all the time**, **without my being consciously aware of it**.

The trouble with the word "unconscious" is that it has all sorts of connotations concerning Sigmund Freud and psychoanalysis. For him, the unconscious was like a dustbin into which you put all those nasty thoughts and feelings that you are frightened or ashamed of. You try to keep the lid on it until you are no longer strong enough, and then you have a nervous breakdown.

But I'm using the word "unconscious" in a quite different sense. I'm describing what's going on, quite normally, in all of us, all the time, without which we'd be overwhelmed by the sheer volume of the things we have to take care of in everyday life.

One example: your physiology. When you've eaten, your body will digest the meal for you. There is simply no way you can help it by trying to become conscious of the digestive process. The best you can do is to facilitate things by, for example, not eating two desserts before sprinting the 400 metres.

Or consider blinking your eye, or scratching an itch, or licking your lips. These are all things that generally happen without your being conscious of what you are doing. If someone throws a brick at you, you duck. You don't first carefully evaluate the alternatives.

Even rather more demanding activities that require learned skills involve the same principle. You can shave, or dress, or tie your shoelaces without having to concentrate on what you're doing. Your body is used to all the necessary actions and will actually carry them out *better* if you're *not* thinking about them. Next time you want to tie your shoelaces, try concentrating. You'll find it much harder.

The same applies to speaking. You use the right words the whole time without having the slightest idea how they happen to pop into your head. If you are asked the name of a five-letter Chinese animal that eats bamboo, "panda" pops up right away. But you've no awareness of how that occurred. Did your mind look in the "China" file first, or in the "Animal" file, or in the "Bamboo Eaters" one? Or, of course, the "Five-Letter" file? We've no idea. It's literally an unconscious process.

Now, think of the really skilful things that you can do without conscious effort.

You can drive from your home to your place of work, perfectly safely, without having to concentrate on every single muscular process involved, even though your mind is absorbed by something else. (Of course, if the unusual or unexpected occurs, your consciousness snaps straight in and you immediately become much more aware, so that you can deal with whatever it is that has happened.)

Or think of something even more complex, like playing the piano. When someone's doing that, they are not consciously thinking which key they have to hit with which finger. Their unconscious knows how to do that.

But only because they practise and practise and practise.

It's the same in sport. Golfers will practise their golf swing, tennis players their backhand, cricketers their ability to catch until these skills become effortless in the sense that no mental input is required.

The top basketball players will shout, "Stop thinking!" to a colleague who is not having a good day, because conscious thought will slow them down.

In acting, the moment you have to think what you are going to say next, there's a little less energy for the acting itself, because it's being siphoned off by the conscious mind for the purpose of remembering.

This intelligent unconscious of ours, then, is astoundingly powerful. It allows us to perform most of our tasks in life without requiring us to concentrate on them. Without it, we couldn't function at all. There'd be much too much to think about.

But that doesn't mean that our intelligent unconscious behaves in an entirely predictable way.

A perfect example. An experimental psychologist in the US asked a group of people to view various Chinese characters that were displayed on a screen, like these:

勠　擦　头　跑　趟

The volunteers were then asked to return a few days later to look at a further batch. Some of the characters they viewed this time around they had seen the week before; others were quite new to them:

东　莞　勠　擦　头　乐　幕

They were asked to say which ones they recognised from the previous session.

The results were, as you would guess, completely hopeless. People had absolutely no clue when it came to recalling these unfamiliar shapes.

Then the psychologists repeated the experiment with a different group. But this time, after the second session, the volunteers were not asked to identify which characters they had seen the week before. They were simply asked to say which ones they liked best.

This may seem a rather odd question, but the group seemed to understand what was required, and were able to say, "Yes, I prefer this character to that character."

And now for the mind-boggling fact . . .

The ones they liked were the ones that they had seen before.

Think about this for a moment. Their unconscious recognised the Chinese characters from the previous week, but instead of prompting the volunteers to say, "Yes, we saw them last week," it simply generated a feeling of liking.

And *that's* the problem with the unconscious. It *is* unconscious. You can't order it about or hit it with a stick. You have to coax it out in all sorts of strange and crafty ways. And be clever about interpreting what it does tell you.

Put simply, you can't ask your unconscious a question, and expect a direct answer—a neat, tidy little verbal message. This is because your unconscious communicates its knowledge to you solely through the *language of the unconscious*.

And **the language of the unconscious is not verbal**. It's like the language of dreams. It shows you images, it gives you feelings, it nudges you around without you immediately knowing what it's getting at.

I'll be coming back to this idea later, because it's so important.

```
*   *   *   *   *   *   *   *   *   *
*   *   *   *   *   *   *   *   *   *
*   *   *   *   *   *   *   *   *   *
*   *   *   *   *   *   *   *   *   *
*   *   *   *   *   *   *   *   *   *
*   *   *   *   *   *   *   *   *   *
*   *   *   *
*   *   *   *           " H a r e
*   *   *   *
*   *   *   *       B r a i n ,
*
*           T o r t o i s e
*
*   *   *   *   *       M i n d "
*   *   *   *   *
*   *   *   *   *   *   *   *   *   *
*   *   *   *   *   *   *   *   *   *
*   *   *   *   *   *   *   *   *   *
*   *   *   *   *   *   *   *   *   *
```

 **the
schools I attended concentrated
entirely on teaching us to think
logically, analytically and verbally
(or numerically).**

But what they *didn't* tell me was
that while this way of thinking is
absolutely right for solving certain
kinds of problems, it's no good at all
for *other* kinds.

This basic truth became much clearer to me when, twenty years ago, I was lucky enough to read a wonderful book by Guy Claxton, called *Hare Brain, Tortoise Mind*.

In it, Guy Claxton talks about two different ways of thinking. The first, he says, involves "figuring matters out, weighing up the pros and cons, constructing arguments and solving problems." He goes on to give various examples: "A mechanic working out why an engine will not fire, a family arguing over the brochures about where to go for next summer's holiday, a scientist trying to interpret an intriguing experimental result, a student wrestling with an examination question: all are employing a way of knowing that relies on reason and logic, on deliberate conscious thinking." He calls this kind of quick, purposeful thinking "Hare Brain."

Then, he argues, there is another kind of thinking which he calls "Tortoise Mind." This, he says, "proceeds more slowly . . . It is often less purposeful and clear-cut, more playful, leisurely or dreamy. In this mode we are ruminating or mulling things over, being contemplative or meditative. We may be pondering a problem, rather than earnestly trying to solve it."

The absolutely crucial point he goes

on to make is that **this leisurely "Tortoise Mind," for all its apparent aimlessness, is just as "intelligent" as the much faster "Hare Brain."** "Recent scientific evidence," he says, "shows convincingly that the more patient, less deliberate modes of mind are particularly suited to making sense of situations that are intricate, shadowy or ill defined . . . when we are not sure what needs to be taken into account, or even which questions to pose—or when the issue is too subtle to be captured by the familiar categories of conscious thought—we need recourse to the tortoise mind . . . This type of intelligence is associated with what we call creativity, or even 'wisdom.'"

Reading this wonderful stuff, I realised that my schools had had such an obsession with logical, critical, analytical thinking that they never appreciated that this kind of mental process is useless if you want to be creative. It was presented as the only way of thinking.

It wasn't until I read Guy Claxton's book that I came to understand the "Tortoise Mind."

So how can we better understand how to think in this slower, more creative way?

My friend Brian Bates, who used to run the Psychology department at the University of Sussex, once told me that during the sixties and seventies some really good research was done on how people can become more creative. But after that, the research generally hit a wall. Because so much of creativity is about the unconscious, there is a limit to what you can say about it!

He did, however, tell me about an experiment of fundamental practical importance that was carried out during the sixties at Berkeley, near San Francisco. A remarkable psychologist called Donald MacKinnon (who had been a spymaster during the Second World War) had become fascinated by creativity, not among artists, but among people like engineers and journalists.

He had a particular interest in architects, because he could see that they needed to be both creative and highly practical. After all, it's no good designing a beautiful building if it's going to fall down.

Donald MacKinnon asked a number of architects whom they considered to be the most creative ones in their profession. Then he went to these "creative" architects and asked them to describe to him what they did, from the moment they got up in the morning to the moment they went to bed at night.

And then he went to a number of uncreative architects (though he didn't tell them that that was why he was talking to them) and asked them exactly the same question.

The conclusion he came to was that there were only two differences between the creative and the uncreative architects.

The first was that **the creative architects knew how to play**.

The second was that **the creative architects always deferred making decisions for as long as they were allowed**.

As philosophers say, let's unpack those two findings.

When MacKinnon talks about "play," he means the ability to get enjoyably absorbed in a puzzle: not just to try to solve it so that you can get on to the next problem, but to become really curious about it for its own sake. He describes this kind of activity as "childlike." Picture small children playing. They are so absorbed in what they are doing that they are not distracted, they're just . . . exploring, not knowing where they're going, and not caring either.

Children at play are totally spontaneous. They are not trying to avoid making mistakes. They don't observe rules. It would be stupid to say to them, "No, you're not doing that right."

At the same time, because their play has no purpose, they feel utterly free from anxiety (perhaps because adults are keeping an eye on the real world for them).

Most adults, by contrast, find it hard to be playful—no doubt because they have to take care of all the responsibilities that come with an adult's life. Creative adults, however, have not forgotten how to play.

Now, let's look at the second characteristic of the creative architects.

Most people are very surprised to learn that this involves deferring decisions for as long as possible. Doesn't this mean that creative architects are, by definition, indecisive? Isn't that a bit impractical and unrealistic?

No!

It simply means they are able to tolerate that vague sense of discomfort that we all feel, when some important decision is left open, because they know that an answer will eventually present itself.

Let me elaborate.

I once wrote a script for a training film about decision-making, and talked to various experts on the subject. They explained to me that if you have a

decision to make, the first question
you must ask is: "When does this
decision have to be made?" You live
in the real world, so there is always a
cut-off point.

But once it's been agreed when that
real-world decision has to happen, why
make it before the deadline arrives?

Why?

Well, it would be foolish, because if
you can wait longer, two incredibly
important things may happen.

1. You may get new information.

2. You may get new ideas.

So why would you make a decision when you don't need to?

Because you're uncomfortable, that's why!

You see, leaving a question unresolved, just leaving it open, makes some people anxious. They worry. And if they can't tolerate that mild discomfort, they go ahead and rush the decision. They probably fool themselves that they're being decisive.

But **creative people are much better at tolerating the vague sense of worry that we all get when we leave something unresolved**.

So if, like the creative architects, you can tolerate that anxiety, you will be able to give yourself the time to come up with a better decision.

NOW . . . the harder part of being creative.

How do we learn to play like a child?

Start with this thought.

The greatest killer of creativity is interruption. It pulls your mind away from what you want to be thinking about. Research has shown that, after an interruption, it can take eight minutes for you to return to your previous state of consciousness, and up to twenty minutes to get back into a state of deep focus.

Let's just think about interruptions . . .

It may be an interruption from outside, like someone coming over and talking to you, or an email popping up in your inbox. Or it may come from inside, as you suddenly remember something that you've forgotten to do, or worry that time is running out, or that you don't think you're clever enough to solve whatever problem it is that you're trying to deal with. (As I was writing this, I heard someone coming down the stairs, and it caused me to lose focus. Then I started to think how often that happens, and the same thing happened again. First, an external interruption, then an internal one.)

But perhaps the biggest interruption coming from your inside is caused by your worrying about making a mistake. This can paralyse you. "Oh," you say to yourself, "I mustn't think that because it might be WRONG."

Let me reassure you. **When you're being creative there is no such thing as a mistake**.

The reason is very simple: you can't possibly know if you are going down a wrong avenue until you've gone down it. So, if you have an idea, you must follow your line of thought to the end to see whether it's likely to be useful or not. You must explore, without necessarily knowing where you're going. As Einstein once pointed out, if we know what we're doing when we're investigating something, then it's not research!

In order to remove such interruptions, whether internal or external, so that you can enter your "Tortoise Mind," you have to create a safe place, where you can play. This involves first creating boundaries of space, and then boundaries of time.

You create boundaries of *space* to stop others interrupting you. You shut the door and put up a "DO NOT DISTURB" sign; or you go and hide somewhere people won't bother you.

You create boundaries of *time*, by arranging, for a specific period, to preserve your boundaries of space. You might, for example, decide to create a specific play period that starts in a few minutes' time and finishes, say, ninety minutes later. You treat those ninety minutes with huge respect and don't allow any interruptions. And, knowing that this chunk of time is sacred, you can then start to play.

Of course, it takes a while before you can do this. The chances are that the first time you try it, you'll find yourself thinking, "Oh, I forgot to call Tom!" Next, you'll remember that you haven't yet bought your cat a birthday present. Then you'll recall how embarrassed you were last night when you couldn't remember your sister's name. Then you'll wonder why your leg is itching so much, and why Germany always wins on penalties, and whether you shouldn't actually start by making yourself a cup of coffee.

Don't worry. It's the same for everyone!

It's just like meditation. The first time you actually sit still, you become aware of something you don't notice when you're dashing around—and that is that your head is full of silly little thoughts and worries. As Hindus say, the mind is like a chattering, drunken monkey. On and on, and all completely trivial and uninvited.

What can you do about this?

Well, people who are stronger-minded than me seem to be able just to bat these thoughts away. Lucky sods. I can't do that. Instead, I write them down straight away on a yellow sticky note on my desk. Then I can forget about them.

Once you start chasing away any distracting thoughts, you'll discover, just like in meditation, that **the longer you sit there**, **the more your mind slows and calms down and settles**. Once that starts to happen you can begin to focus on the problem you've chosen to think about. You just keep it vaguely there, in your mind, while you let your thoughts wander around.

In order to avoid allowing them to wander too far, you could take a tip from my great friend, the Oscar-winning screenwriter Bill Goldman. (*Butch Cassidy and the Sundance Kid*, *All the President's Men*, *The Princess Bride*, *Misery*, *A Bridge Too Far*, *The Great Waldo Pepper*, *The Hot Rock*, *Marathon Man*—need I say more?) He once told me that when he was working on a particular scene he'd write down the key idea behind it on a piece of paper, and then stick the note right in front of his nose on the computer. If he realised his mind had wandered too far, he would glance at the note and that would bring him back to what he was trying to achieve.

So you just sit there and, eventually, as the mind quietens, odd ideas and notions relevant to your puzzle start popping in your mind. But they are . . . *odd*!

And the reason they seem odd is that they're not what our usual logical, criti-cal, analytical mind is used to. They don't arrive in the form of words, in neatly typed little sentences. Because they come from your unconscious, they speak the language of the unconscious.

You will remember that I've touched on this before.

Think about how you think when you're not conscious, when you're asleep. Consider your dreams. When you recall your dreams, you remember situations, you remember images, you remember feelings, you remember recurring patterns . . . but nothing is very clear-cut or precise.

Now, if you find all this a bit "touchy-feely," read what Einstein had to say on the subject of ideas:

"The words or the language, as they are written or spoken," he wrote, "do not seem to play any role in my mechanism of thought. The psychical entities which seem to serve as elements in thought are certain signs and more or less clear images which can be 'voluntarily' reproduced and combined . . . this combinatory play seems to be the essential feature in productive thought—before there is any connection with logical construction in words or other kinds of signs which can be communicated to others."

The fact is that when you're playing with images and feelings, you never know where a vital prompting may come from. Take August Kekule von Stradonitz, the German organic chemist who discovered the structure of benzene. Once, late at night, he was sitting, staring into the fire. It was an old-fashioned wood fire so there were flames licking around in all directions. As he gazed, they started to look like snakes in his imagination. The more he gazed into the fire in this sleepy, relaxed kind of way, the more they began to look like snakes that were biting their own tails. And as he sat there, half-asleep, it suddenly occurred to him that the snake biting its own tail was a ring— and that so too was the structure of a benzene molecule.

And, if your logical, analytical "Hare Brain" senses that you're wandering too

far away and that hard, logical thinking should be in there *somewhere* . . .

Then think of one of the greatest
scientists of all time, Edison, the
man who invented the light bulb. He
found that he got his best ideas in that
funny no man's land between being
awake and being asleep. So he used
to sit in a comfy armchair with a few
ball bearings in his hand and a metal
bowl underneath. When he dropped
off to sleep his hand relaxed, the ball
bearings fell on to the plate and the
noise they made woke him up. He'd
then pick up the ball bearings again
and sit back and get into that same
drowsy, dreamy frame of mind that
he'd just been in.

So when we are in touch with our unconscious, it sends us hints and gentle nudges, and *that's* why we have to be quiet. That's why we're practising a kind of meditation. Because if we don't, if instead we are running around, looking at our watches and checking our smartphones, there's not a hope in hell that we're going to notice the subtle messages we're being sent.

A word of warning. **When we're trying to be creative, there's a real lack of clarity during most of the process**. Our rational, analytical mind, of course, loves clarity—in fact, it *worships* it. But at the start of the creative process things cannot be clear. They are bound to be confusing. If it's a new thought,

how can you possibly understand it
straight away? You've never been there
before. It feels unfamiliar. So, much of
our "Tortoise Mind" work takes place
in an atmosphere of uncertainty and
gentle confusion.

It's therefore really important that
you don't rush. **Let these new notions
of yours slowly become clearer**, **and
clearer**, **and clearer**. Real clarity will
eventually emerge.

And at that point you'll have . . . a
new idea!

Notice that I did not say "a new good
idea." It might be a terrible one. It
might be brilliant.

So how do you decide which it is, or whether, in fact, it's a bit of both?

Because what you do at this point, when this new idea of yours has become pretty clear, is to bring in your critical, analytical, fact-seeking mind to assess it.

Yes, your "Hare Brain," which has been sitting around twiddling its ears, can now hop in and apply all its hard-nosed "scientific" thinking: gathering data, making measurements, reaching logical conclusions, generally checking out your new idea . . . *and seeing if it will actually fly.*

Yes? No? Or . . . perhaps?

It might be an idea with both good bits and not-so-good bits. If that's the case, once you've decided with your logical mind which parts you want to keep, and which you can now get rid of, you can later go back into your creative mood again, and build on the good parts.

It is, however, very important that **when you first have a new idea**, **you don't get critical too soon**. New and "woolly" ideas shouldn't be attacked by your logical brain until they've had time to grow, to become clearer and sturdier. New ideas are rather like small creatures. They're easily strangled.

So exercise patience, until you have

a clear sense of what it is that you've come up with. Then you can bring your critical thinking in. Not before.

There's quite a good way of telling when your creative period has done its job and it's time to move on. If you find that you've had lots of vague new ideas and are starting to feel a bit overwhelmed and confused, that's the moment to start work on clarifying them, prior to bringing your logical thinking to bear.

Now you're in a logical, critical period. After a time there, however, when you've assessed everything, you will get a bit *bored*. That's a sign that now is the moment to go back into your creative thinking mode again. And so you go backwards and forwards between the creative mode of thinking and the analytical mode of thinking until, finally, you get to something that's a bit special.

This back-and-forth process is called iteration. It's what creative people do all the time.

And it's what I did when I was writing the screenplay for *A Fish Called Wanda*. I went through draft after draft, using my "Tortoise Mind" to come up with ideas and resolve problems, and my "Hare Brain" to clarify my thoughts and sort out logical inconsistencies. In the end, it took thirteen drafts, but I knew it was worth it because each time the screenplay became that little better. And the end result was the only writing award I've ever won!

"Tortoise Mind."

"Hare Brain."

They need each other.

But keep them separate!

Hints and Suggestions

in this section, I am drawing on my experience as a writer. However, people who do very different things—from artists to psychiatrists and from musicians to inventors—tell me that the mental processes they go through to come up with new ideas are similar to the ones I employ. I hope, therefore, that the following rather random thoughts about writing may be useful to people creating in other fields.

* * * * * * * * * *

"Write about what you know"

* * * * * * * * * *

First-time authors are often told: "Write about what you know." It's a piece of advice that reminds me of a sign you often see at the end of London Underground carriages: "Lower window for ventilation." In other words, it falls into the category of "the Bleedin' Obvious." I mean, is it likely you would think, "Well, I know absolutely nothing about wasp farming in North Dakota, so I'll make the hero of my first novel a wasp farmer in Bismarck"? Or, "As I've always worked on a commercial fishing boat, I'm going to write a biography of a famous Indonesian temple dancer"? Of course you must write what you know about. Then, if you become successful and really want to write about a subject you have absolutely no knowledge of, you can do a lot of research first. (If you really, really want to.)

I think this basic rule applies everywhere: you are most likely to be creative in an area that you already know and care about.

Looking for inspiration

When you start something creative for the first time, you have no idea what you are doing! But, whether you're writing or painting or composing a song, you do need to start with an idea. As a beginner it's not very likely that you'll come up with a very good one. So "borrow" an idea from someone you admire—an idea that really appeals to you personally. If you start working on that, you'll make it your own as you play with it. You're learning, and learning from something or someone you admire is not stealing. It's called "being influenced by."

Of course, that doesn't mean you can slavishly copy exactly what another person has done. That is stealing. And, in any case, what would be the point of doing that if you're trying to produce something creative? Exact copying can teach technique, but this little book is about creativity, not forgery!

If you find the notion of borrowing like this a bit dodgy, look up a fellow called

Shakespeare. He stole all his plots, and then wrote rather creatively.

* * * * * * * * * *

Making an imaginative leap

* * * * * * * * * *

The key word here is "leap." A leap
sounds like a very big jump. But
suppose the "leap" is only a hop. Or
a skip. Or a hop, a skip and a jump?
A very tiny hop, like moving a rose to
the middle of a flower arrangement,
is only a teeny, tiny bit creative.
Whereas Einstein's Theory of Relativity

is probably the winner of the title "Greatest Scientific Long Jump Ever."

The general principle is this: the bigger the leap, the longer the creative period is likely to be.

If you're writing creatively, you can improve scripts hugely by making lots of smaller improvements that aren't very creative at all. At other times, you may think of a major addition, or change, such as when Steven Spielberg realised during the making of *Jaws* that the audience did not need to keep seeing the shark. Remember, the unconscious is totally unpredictable. Many Nobel Prize winners report that their breakthrough came completely out of the blue. After years of pondering, it just . . . popped into their minds. Some even feel they don't really deserve their prize, as their idea was "given" to them, without them feeling they'd really produced it themselves!

* * * * * * * * * *

Keeping going

* * * * * * * * * *

If you want to be creative in the world of science or architecture or medicine, you have to spend years educating yourself before you are ready to start thinking creatively about anything your colleagues might not already know.

However, in the Arts, it sometimes happens that successful novelists never quite achieve the originality of their first novel. This is because beginners sometimes have a freshness in their approach that later fades away. Picasso said that he drew better when he was ten than he ever did again. Edvard Munch's later paintings never recaptured the intensity of his earliest ones.

The Buddhists have a phrase for this—"Beginner's Mind"—expressing how experience can be more vivid when it's not dulled by familiarity. It's the psychological equivalent of the Law of Diminishing Returns. This is why even the very best minds seem to produce work that can divide itself into three stages. First, they produce original work as they learn their craft; second, when they've mastered their craft, they begin to express their mature ideas in their best works; third, there's a tailing-off of their powers, as their insights become more familiar.

It seems that it's rare for someone creative to maintain a constant high level of freshness. Many people, in the course of acquiring great understanding and knowledge of a subject, become conventional in their thinking. Others, like Richard Feynman, the theoretical physicist, manage never to lose their ability to come up with fresh ideas. In other words, they learn to nurture their unconscious, and to trust it. Feynman spent a lot of time playing the drums. The great mathematician John Conway spent much of his time playing games.

Playing . . . keeps you "fresh."

* * * * * * * * * *

Coping with setbacks

* * * * * * * * * *

Whenever you try to come up with something original, you will find that some days the stuff flows, and some days it doesn't. When Graham Chapman and I started writing together we would get terribly frustrated and despairing when we hit a fallow period—sometimes a whole morning or even a day when we produced nothing really good. But then we noticed that, despite this, we had a consistent average: every week we wrote about fifteen to eighteen minutes of good stuff. All we had to do was to sit there, whether it flowed or it didn't, and by Friday evening we would have enough. We came to understand that the blockages weren't an interruption in the process, they were part of it. For example, when you eat, the bit where the fork returns empty to your plate isn't a failure. It's just part of the eating process.

The anthropologist Gregory Bateson once said, "You can't have a new idea 'til you've got rid of an old one."

This insight helped me to view my fallow periods as preparatory to the fertile ones, and therefore as an inseparable part of the whole creative process. When the juices are not flowing, don't beat yourself up and wonder if you should retrain as a priest. Just sit around and play, until your unconscious is ready to cough up some stuff. Getting discouraged is a total waste of your time.

* * * * * * * * * *

Get your panic in early

* * * * * * * * * *

My experience is that whenever I'm faced with a difficult problem, I sense a pang of fear. It's straightforward terror that I may not be able to solve whatever it is that I'm wrestling with. And writing is difficult. Let me rephrase that. Writing is easy. Writing well is difficult. (A friend of mine was in a restaurant with his little boy when

Harold Pinter walked in. He told his son, "That's Harold Pinter. He's a very fine writer." The boy replied, "Ooh! Can he do W's?")

So if, like me, you feel a little bit rattled as you face your challenge, here's my advice: get your panic in early! The good thing about panic is that it gives you energy. You never think, "I'm panicking, so I'll have a nice snooze." Instead, the panic will help you get down to the job.

But don't expect to solve anything for ages. Just begin to make a few notes, knowing they don't have to be any good, and you will throw them away soon. Apart from anything else, this will help you to calm down, because if you have zero expectations at the start, you can hardly fail. And you're already priming your unconscious . . .

The key thing is to start, even if it feels as though you're forcing yourself through an emotional roadblock.

Begin with simple stuff, such as . . . Who are you writing for? You might be writing for academics, in which case you don't have to be interesting. Or for people who have a limited attention span, in which case you have to be *very* interesting. Then, you can ask yourself whether the audience will easily accept what you're saying, or whether they might be resistant. If so, you'll have to persuade them, and not just tell them.

Then you can start pondering, "What am I really trying to say?" "What is the point of this piece of journalism, or speech, or book, or play, or pamphlet, or email?" Think up different approaches, compare them, begin gathering key facts and research—it never does any harm to have a few quotes! And—in case you haven't realised this yet—recognise that all this time you will be feeding your unconscious and it will be chewing everything over the moment you stop working. Which is why, if you now go for a walk, by the time you get back, you'll have a couple more ideas to add to your notes.

Finally . . . as you get further into this piece of writing, remember just one thing: "Brevity is the soul of wit." It is also the soul of not boring people. Remember the famous apology, "Sorry this is such a long letter, but I didn't have time to write a shorter one." So when you finish your first draft:

1. Cut anything that is not relevant (there will be more than you think).

2. Don't repeat yourself unless you really want to.

Good luck. And get started.

* * * * * * * * * *

Your thoughts follow your mood

* * * * * * * * * *

When my friend Professor Brian Bates pointed this out to me decades ago, it came as a complete revelation. And yet . . . it's so obvious! How could I not have noticed something that was staring me in the face? We all know that, if we're depressed, we don't have cheerful, optimistic, energetic thoughts.

And if we are happy, we can't take gloomy, pessimistic thoughts seriously. If we're angry, we don't want to play with the kittens—we want to plot our revenge. If we're anxious, we worry. If we're full of ourselves, we feel decisive. If we're feeling envious, we can't enjoy other people's success much.

Now, feeling creative isn't exactly an emotion. It's a frame of mind. But if you're in the wrong frame of mind— if you're distracted or worrying about something else—it follows that you're not going to be creative.

* * * * * * * * * *

The dangers of over-confidence

* * * * * * * * * *

As a general rule, when people become absolutely certain that they know what they're doing, their creativity plummets. This is because they think they have nothing more to learn. Once they believe this, they naturally stop learning and fall back on established patterns. And that means they don't grow.

The trouble is that most people want to *be* right. The very best people, however, want to know *if* they're right. That's the great thing about working in comedy. If the audience doesn't laugh, you know you've got it wrong.

* * * * * * * * * *

Testing your idea

* * * * * * * * * *

Once you've come up with a new idea,
there are two ways to test it. First,
there is the one I described earlier,
when you bring the critical facul-
ties you suspended during the playful
stage to bear on whatever it is that
you have thought of. You're now suffi-
ciently clear about your idea to be in

a position to evaluate it. If you decide it can be improved, you go into the iteration process, until you are really satisfied with it. This, of course, involves making assessments, but if you are curious and keen to learn, the more experience you gain, the better your judgement will become. Of course, you'll inevitably make some mistakes, but even these will help hone your skills for the future.

Second, when you're sure that you really like your new idea, you can proceed from thinking to doing, from planning to action. This might be a small step, or a huge one. If you've designed a car, moving on to actually producing it may be a bit demanding (less so if you're the head designer at the Ford factory). If you've designed a dress, getting it made may be more immediately feasible, in which case you can then try it on and see how much you like it. If you've finally finished a book or a painting, you can show it to people who you think have good judgement and see if their opinions affect what you think of it. If you're a soldier, and you've made your battle plan, you just carry out the attack (stopping to ask for feedback on the plan isn't going to help). If you've written a script, you will have to find a producer who likes it enough to want to get it made. (At which point you need to prepare for more iteration!)

* * * * * * * * * *

Kill your darlings

* * * * * * * * * *

On one occasion, when my friend the
great screenwriter Bill Goldman was
helping me with a script, he advised
me to "kill my darlings," a phrase
he said he'd borrowed from William
Faulkner. I was slightly taken aback,
but I think I now understand what he
meant rather better than I did at the
time! His point was that any good

work of art will change—sometimes in major ways—during the course of its creation. At the beginning of the process a writer may get a great idea—one that they particularly like. This is their "darling." Inevitably, as the project develops, parts of the story will change and that "darling" may not fit well into the new version of the narrative. A good writer will jettison it. A less good writer will hang on to it, so hindering the transition of the story to its new form. I've noticed that younger writers tend to cling to their darlings. Those who are more experienced have got so used to redrafting and rewriting that they find it easier to let them die. They are, quite simply, more murderous.

Seeking a second opinion

If you are an experienced writer, and you show people your work, there are four questions you need to ask:

1. Where were you bored?

2. Where could you not understand what was going on?

3. Where did you not find things credible?

4. Was there anything that you found emotionally confusing?

Once you have the answers to these, then you go away, decide how valid the problems are . . . and *fix them yourself*. The people you have asked will probably suggest their solutions too. Ignore these completely. Smile, look interested, thank them and leave, because they have no idea what they're talking about. Unless they are writers themselves. Then . . . listen carefully. But at the end of the day, you and only you must decide which criticisms and suggestions you accept.

While you're considering all this don't ask yourself who is right. Ask which idea is better.

As to when you should seek a second opinion, my view is that you should do so when you have reached a point of sufficient clarity for someone else's judgement to be of practical help.

Don't wait until you feel your idea or project is as good as possible, because you may waste a lot of time if you ask for feedback too late in the procedure. If I'm writing a speech, I'll ask four or five individuals what they think of my first draft. That way I immediately find out what grabs people and what doesn't.

My second draft might be as much as fifty per cent different. I show the second draft to two or three new readers to get a fresh view. And this iteration process goes on until I'm satisfied with the responses I am receiving. Sometimes I send the final draft to those who looked at it first time around. Almost inevitably they will say, with some surprise, "Oh! It's much better!"

I wonder why.

If you're writing a narrative, tell the rough outline to someone. Take note of when they lose interest. That's where the story's gone wrong! Next time you tell it, just hope you get further along before people's attention drifts . . .

* * * * * * * * * *

* * * * * * * * * *

* * * * * * * * * *

* * * * * * * * * *

* * * * * * * * * *

* * * * * * * * * *

*   *

*   *Other books*   *

*   *

* * *   *by*   * * *

*   *

*   *John Cleese*   *

*   *

* * * * * * * * * *

* * * * * * * * * *

* * * * * * * * * *

* * * * * * * * * *

* * * * * * * * * *

* * * * * * * * * *

Families and How to Survive Them
(with Dr. Robin Skynner)

Life and How to Survive It
(with Dr. Robin Skynner)

So, Anyway...
The Autobiography

Professor at Large:
The Cornell Years